T0405808

BEATING
HOSPITAL GRADE
DEPRESSION
AND ANXIETY

A Lived Experience Guide to
Recovering Your Body, Mind and Spirit

W.B. TURNER

Copyright © 2025 by W.B. Turner

All rights reserved. No part of this publication may be reproduced, distributed or transmitted in any form or by any means, including photocopying, recording, or other electronic or mechanical methods, without the prior written permission of the publisher, except in the case of brief quotations embodied in critical reviews and certain other non-commercial uses permitted by copyright law. All enquiries should be made to will@wbturner.com.

ISBN: 978-1-76385-240-2 (paperback), 978-1-76385-241-9 (ebook)

Scriptures taken from the Holy Bible, New International Version®, NIV®. Copyright © 1973, 1978, 1984, 2011 by Biblica, Inc.™ Used by permission of Zondervan. All rights reserved worldwide. www.zondervan.com The "NIV" and "New International Version" are trademarks registered in the United States Patent and Trademark Office by Biblica, Inc.™

DISCLAIMER: The content presented in this book is provided for inspiration and informational purposes only and should not be used to replace the specialised training and professional judgement of a healthcare or mental healthcare professional. The author and publisher claim no responsibility or liability to any person or entity, arising directly or indirectly from any person taking or not taking action based on the information in this book.

GET THE AUDIOBOOK
FOR FREE!

To say thanks for purchasing my book, I would like to give you the Audiobook version 100% FREE!

I know you're more likely to finish this book if you have the Audiobook. Get your free copy by visiting

WBTURNER.COM

Dedication

To my children, Elijah, Siena, Jesse and Leo. May you always treasure your mental health.

CONTENTS

Preface 1

Introduction 3

Part 1 The Breakdown 7

Chapter 1:   My Pre-Diagnosis Roller-Coaster 8

Chapter 2:   A Positive Psychiatric Hospital Experience 16

Part 2 The Body 21

Chapter 3:   Nutrition 23

Chapter 4:   Exercise 30

Chapter 5:   Sleep 33

Chapter 6:   Medication and Side Effects 37

Part 3 The Mind 41

Chapter 7:   Six Strategies to Counter Depression 42

Chapter 8:   Six Strategies to Counter Anxiety 48

Part 4 The Spirit 57

Chapter 9:   Prayer 59

Chapter 10: Worship and Community 63

Chapter 11: Spiritual Reading 65

Chapter 12: Inspiration 69

Chapter 13: Go Forth 76

About the Author 79

PREFACE

When I was a young adult, I nearly died during a three-year period where I was unknowingly suffering from a severe mental illness. Thankfully, during an eight-week stay in a psychiatric hospital, I was finally accurately diagnosed. What followed was a long journey of recovery.

Looking back, I realise what would have helped my recovery was a book written by someone with lived experience of what I was going through.

Books about mental health written by doctors and psychologists had their place in my recovery journey. However, I rarely read them from cover to cover because they were so dense, and a "workbook" (as many of them are framed) is not very enticing to someone who can barely get out of bed in the morning because of their mental troubles.

When I think about the factors that contributed to my recovery and ongoing well-being, the advice I have received from doctors is but part of a much greater whole. This is not to discount the vital importance of medical professionals in treating those who have a mental illness. It is simply an acknowledgement that so much more goes into a successful recovery than the clinical.

As someone with lived experience of both a mood disorder (bipolar disorder) and an anxiety disorder (obsessive-compulsive disorder), my motivation for writing this book is to provide an angle for those who need help with knowing how to come to terms and live confidently with a mental illness from someone who has been through it themselves.

I am not a clinician; my expertise lies in my lived experience and the insights I have gained through more than two decades that began with a significant breakdown involving hospitalisation, a long recovery process, and learning how to maintain my mental health as someone who now works full-time and has a wife and four children.

In these pages, I use my own experience as a field study in life after a major mental breakdown, and I hope it can be a valuable resource for anyone whose experience bears some resemblance to mine.

If that is you, I believe this book can help speed up your recovery and save you unnecessary time and stress.

INTRODUCTION

For me, coming to grips with having a psychotic condition didn't quite work like flicking a switch. It was more like a pendulum between a fully delusional state and one where I could see my illness for what it was.

This took place when I was admitted to a psychiatric hospital twenty years ago. Most of my first week was spent at the delusional end of the spectrum, which manifested itself as a firm conviction that I was a fraud.

I remember writing and handing a note to one of the nurses because I was too ashamed to tell them myself. It said I had orchestrated my admission so that I could prey on vulnerable inpatients.

I expected to be taken away and locked up, never to see my family or friends again.

On another occasion, after playing a friendly game of pool with another inpatient, I withdrew to my room feeling deeply remorseful because I had acted in a friendly manner that, in some inverted way, must have been intended to cause him spiritual harm.

I recall my eldest brother Matthew phoning in to see how I was doing. Afterwards, I asked my dad to suggest he doesn't call again because I believed I could somehow cause harm to him, his wife and his newborn baby simply by having a normal conversation with him over the phone.

I then shared with my dad that I was a fraud and not really ill. Just like the nurse a few days before, he gently acknowledged my point of view several times (I was very insistent) and said that, for now, the hospital was the best place for me to be.

Within a week of my hospital admission, my doctor put the pieces together. She said I was experiencing a double whammy of obsessive thoughts and severe depression that was causing the delusions.

She made a diagnosis of bipolar disorder type 1 and obsessive-compulsive disorder (OCD).

I don't remember what my initial reaction was, but a day or two later, in the hospital lounge, I was reading a pamphlet about bipolar disorder and the back cover of a book about OCD called *When Perfect Isn't Good Enough*. As I read the content, I felt like I was looking in a mirror.

I began to understand the past three years of my life in an entirely new light.

That same evening, my brother Henry came to visit, and we chewed over the diagnosis of bipolar disorder, and I shared with him about reading the pamphlet. He said he also had been doing some reading and wondered whether something was going awry with how my brain had been interacting with my conscience.

As is often the case in life, it took a relational moment like this one to cement in my own mind that I had indeed been suffering quite severely from a mental illness. After Henry left, I had a strong feeling of gratitude and knelt and prayed with a clear mind for the first time in months, knowing that my recovery was now underway.

From the point of first grasping my diagnosis, it would take another seven weeks for me to be stable enough to be ready for discharge.

Over this time, much work had to be done to get me from that first glimpse of clarity to having a reasonable level of mental stability.

There were three aspects to my hospital treatment.

The first was finding the suitable types and levels of medication to counter the neurological problems that contributed to me being in the state I was in.

The second was group and individual therapy sessions, where I became educated about my illness and began learning the skills to bring it under control and function healthily.

The third aspect was the care of the hospital staff, visits from family and friends, and the company of other inpatients as I began to find my feet again.

Another breakthrough moment happened during week two or three of my stay. I had been learning about mindfulness, which had been explained to me in some group therapy sessions.

I sat down to practice a simple exercise involving focusing on my senses. I trained my attention on a series of five different objects in my field of vision, then five sounds to my ears, then five parts of my body, and cycled through the pattern repeatedly.

It had a remarkable circuit-breaking effect on my obsessive thoughts.

Through this exercise and others like it, I began to regain my sanity because I was training my mind to be fully present—something it had not done for months or perhaps years.

I liken the start of my recovery to the launch of a space shuttle. Tremendous amounts of energy go into getting it off the ground, and its many parts must work together.

To continue with the space image, in the late 1970s, NASA launched the space probe Voyager into the solar system to take pictures of the outer planets. To achieve the mission, it had a certain amount of power it could direct into changing course, but a critical factor in its journey was how it harnessed the gravity of the planets it visited along the way. They worked as a slingshot to propel the probe from planet to planet and then into outer space, where it continues its interstellar mission to this day.

We humans are not so different. We all need to leverage power external to ourselves to get where we want to go in life's journey. The make-up of these power sources may differ according to one's personality and needs, but they all apply to the three elements of body, mind and spirit that form my framework for a successful recovery.

1. Body

Recovery begins with caring for the whole body, from head to toe. I emphasise the "body basics" of nutrition, exercise and sleep. These fundamentals are crucial for maximising energy levels. By optimising these areas, it is easier to conserve, replenish and direct both physical and mental energy, which is vital for a thorough recovery and maintaining ongoing wellness.

2. Mind

How you think goes a long way in determining how mentally healthy you are. For this reason, improving and strengthening your mindset is key to resilience during life's inevitable difficulties. Although depression and anxiety often overlap, I address them separately in this part of the book to highlight the specific strategies that have helped me manage and overcome each of these conditions.

3. Spirit

The spiritual aspect, often overlooked in discussions about mental health, is in my view central to every person's needs. For me, my Christian faith plays a significant role. In this part of the book, I discuss not only faith but also relationships and sources of inspiration such as movies—things not typically categorised as "spiritual" but which are nonetheless means of cultivating inner peace and motivation for life.

It can be daunting to know exactly *where* to start when embarking on a recovery. I think it's a case of keeping it simple and taking things one step at a time, and this book is designed to help you with that in very practical ways.

Sitting in my hospital room doing the mindfulness exercise, I realised that my starting point was to do whatever was needed to maintain a stable mood.

Everything else came second.

My hope is that, as a fellow traveller, these meditations from my emergency can provide you guidance for your own journey of recovery to better mental health.

PART 1
THE BREAKDOWN

CHAPTER 1
MY PRE-DIAGNOSIS ROLLER-COASTER

Tell me not, in mournful numbers,
Life is but an empty dream!
For the soul is dead that slumbers,
And things are not what they seem.

– Henry Wadsworth Longfellow, 'A Psalm of Life'

So, how did I come to be in the mental state I was in when I was admitted to hospital?

The preceding three years were bookended by two events that changed the world as I knew it. The first was the terrorist attacks of September 11, 2001. The other was living and working on my family's farm during an extreme drought in the winter of 2004.

Yet, traumatic as they were, those experiences in themselves were not solely to blame for bringing me to a psychiatric hospital. What had been going on inside me was the vital ingredient.

In 2001, I was eighteen years old and had graduated from high school the year before, so it was naturally a period of change in my life, just like it is for anyone leaving school. My final year of school in 2000 was intense, and I threw myself into studying for the leaving exams.

Owing to the privileged boarding school I attended, there were no obstructions, such as part-time work, to get in the way of achieving the highest possible score I could. While I had good friendships at school, I didn't spend much time socialising.

I decided to sign up for a cadetship with a "big four" professional services firm, which I started early in 2001, not long after finishing the school leaving exams. It involved full-time work, attending university at night and studying part-time. Like my final year of school, there was not much downtime built into my new routine, which also involved living in the "real world" of renting and paying my own way for the first time.

While I did enjoy the familiarity of sharing an apartment with my older sister that year, the intense routine of work and study had the effect of isolating me socially while many of my friends were having a wonderful time at university or taking a year off to decide what they would do next.

The week before I began the cadetship, a good friend from school was tragically killed in a car-train collision. It came as a profound shock at a point where I was already dealing with plenty of change.

As the year progressed, I felt exhausted from the heavy load of work, study and lack of social connection.

Since my friend's sudden death, I had been confronted by my own mortality and was pondering the big questions about life and eternity. While at a school camp in my mid-teens, I prayed with a friend from a strong Pentecostal family and committed myself to faith in Jesus Christ. It was a life-changing moment for me where I was squaring up with what I had believed to be true for as long as I could remember but had not previously owned for myself. In the time since making that commitment, I had become lukewarm in my faith and felt conscious of the distance between myself and God.

Early in the morning of September 12, 2001 (Sydney time), I awoke to my regular routine of getting up, making breakfast and preparing for work. I switched on my usual radio breakfast show and instantly noticed a different demeanour from the usually chirpy hosts.

Instinctively, I went to the living room and turned on the television. An American news anchor was speaking, and behind him was the late afternoon skyline of New York City. Something was wrong with what I was seeing. Smoke was billowing from Lower Manhattan.

What I saw next confirmed the rising dread I felt: a series of still images of a jet plane crashing into one of the Twin Towers, the same building I had stood on top of a couple of years earlier as an excited teenager while on a student exchange program.

What followed was a recap of what had happened some seven hours earlier, but it was fresh to my eyes because I had been sound asleep when it all happened. As both World Trade Center towers crumbled before my eyes, it may as well have been live.

Physically, I was shaking and felt that I was about to die. Thoughts and images came quickly, unregulated by reason and totally horrifying. I was alone and beyond help, or so it seemed. What I felt was desperation, wishing I could undo whatever it was I had done wrong to cause my life to be ending. Next, I imagined myself in a jungle somewhere with an automatic rifle: a conscript in the armed forces fighting whichever country or axis was behind the attacks.

I looked out the window from my apartment and saw a woman in the neighbouring high-rise block shaking a dusty rug out of her window. I wondered who could be doing something so mundane when the world seemed to be collapsing. It was the jolt of reality that returned me to earth. It's an image that has stayed with me ever since.

In the ensuing months, I would come to learn that what I experienced that morning was a panic attack. In a lot of ways, a panic attack is an internal earthquake. After experiencing it, the mind becomes cracked and traumatised. And much like seismic activity, it leaves a person's mental terrain fractured and fragile. On top of all this, there are aftershocks—fresh panic attacks to return and terrify the person affected, complete with their sensations of impending doom.

To give you a sense of how debilitating they can be, I remember some weeks after 9/11 I was at a restaurant having dinner with someone I had been dating. In the middle of a conversation with her, quite suddenly, I was gripped by another one of these attacks. My body became rigid, and I could not speak for what must have been five minutes. Quite understandably, she didn't want to keep dating me after that experience.

Although I did seek help for what I was going through and began seeing a psychiatrist that our family doctor recommended, unfortunately he (the psychiatrist) wasn't a very good one. Apart from identifying the panic attacks, the psychiatrist never gave me a clear diagnosis despite prescribing a series of medications, including (I would learn much later) antipsychotics, to treat my mental problems.

As the following year (2002) began, I quit the cadetship and switched to full-time study, which included living on campus at a residential college at the University of Sydney. With a new-found resolve to be committed to my faith, I began regularly attending an evangelical Anglican church and was part of a Bible study group.

The church community was young and vibrant, the preaching was engaging, and I relished the theology as much as the social aspect.

Although the panic attacks subsided that year, my mental illness developed into a series of depressive episodes fuelled by obsessive thoughts and compulsive behaviours with strong religious themes.

One theme was concern about my own perilous standing before God. This fear centred on my faulty interpretation of two biblical concepts I had come across.

The first concept was Jesus' reference in the Gospels to blasphemy against the Holy Spirit, which he says, "will not be forgiven, either in this age or in the age to come" (Matthew 12:32). The other was a concept which came up in the Bible study group. Chapter 6 of the book of Hebrews talks about someone who has "fallen away" being unable "to be brought back to repentance" because "they are crucifying the Son of God all over again". Both concepts triggered within me a fear of stepping past a hell-bound point of no return.

The other theme that caused me mental anguish was a preoccupation with others' standing before God considering what the Bible says about predestination. This was an entirely new idea to me, one that had come up in church and Bible study that year. Predestination is something referred to in a few places in Saint Paul's New Testament letters, which I interpreted through a Calvinist lens. This led me to believe those around me could be doomed to hell due to the Almighty's predetermined decision about them. The Bible verse that appeared to state this most clearly was from chapter 9 of Paul's letter to the Romans:

Rebekah's children were conceived at the same time by our father Isaac. Yet, before the twins were born or had done anything good or bad—in order that God's purpose in election might stand: not by works but by him who calls—she was told, 'The older will serve the younger.' Just as it is written: 'Jacob I loved, but Esau I hated.'

The fear about my cliffhanger standing before God drove my anxiety, and my fear for others fed the depression because I was so shocked to learn that, apparently, God didn't love everyone like I had always been taught at school. Instead, he seemed to love some and hate others even before they were born.

The catch-22 in all of this was that because I feared saying something unforgivable, I could not articulate to anyone what was troubling me so much about these religious beliefs. This served to reinforce my internalisation of these problems and the downward spiral of anxiety and depression I experienced.

From an OCD perspective, I became meticulous about my behaviour, and this expression of OCD is commonly referred to as "Scrupulosity". A few examples give a flavour of what this looked like.

One day, during an English literature class, the professor teaching the course picked up my copy of *The English Patient* from my desk to read an excerpt from it. It was quite a normal occurrence in a class like that, but I emailed him later to apologise because I explained that I had sometimes been reading the book when using the bathroom, and I was concerned about the hygiene of him having touched the book.

On another occasion, during a midterm economics exam, I finished the paragraph I was writing after the lecturer called for "pens down." After everyone else had left the hall, I told the lecturer about it and asked that I be penalised.

During a semester break, I took a holiday job at a grocery store. One of my tasks was to bag carrots for display. I took an exceptionally long time because I would check every single carrot for any sign of rot or other imperfection, and the store owner was not impressed with my productivity.

I could give dozens more examples, but you get the picture.

Around this time, I began to obsess about the predetermined eternal destiny of people around me. It was a torturous experience having regular conversations with people while at the same time imagining them in hell.

It led to significant pauses in my speech as I tried to continue the conversation with whoever I was talking to while, at the same time, screening my words for any sign of blasphemy due to the strong negative emotions I was feeling towards God.

I remember being at a party on campus and being introduced to someone. They told me their name, and it must have taken about 15 seconds for me to respond with, "My name is Will."

They must have thought I was on drugs, and in an important sense, I was. The psychiatrist must have suspected me of experiencing psychosis because he prescribed me a potent antipsychotic with strong sedative qualities and a powerful side effect of making me ravenous (I say this all in hindsight—I was not made aware of any of this at the time).

On that drug, I remember sleeping like I had never slept before and finding it challenging to stay awake in lectures, particularly ones between breakfast and lunch. Speaking of meals, I began to eat about twice as much as usual, and I gained so much weight that I broke a bone in my foot.

Owing to the lack of positive results with psychiatry, my mum had been investigating what else might help. She came across something called Emotional Freedom Techniques, an alternative therapy that involves tapping specific points on the body while focusing on negative emotions or physical sensations. Based on the principles of acupuncture, it is believed to balance the body's energy and release blocked emotions, reducing stress and promoting emotional healing.

What happened next was one of the most remarkable experiences of my life. During the EFT appointment, the practitioner asked me basic questions about what was on my mind while tapping a series of points on my hand, face and lower neck.

I felt comfortable articulating what was troubling me about the concept of predestination, and immediately, I felt some emotional relief. That night after the appointment, I remember not sleeping particularly well, as if my mind and body had been given a shake like a snow globe.

The following day, I took myself to a barber shop for a haircut. I was aware of the pleasant smell of the hair products, the feel of the barber doing his work on my hair, and the music playing on the shop radio. It was a song by the Dixie Chicks called *Landslide*, and the sweet harmony of the three female voices stirred positive emotions I had not felt in months.

After the haircut, I decided to jog lightly back to campus. It had been about eight weeks since my foot fracture, and this was the first time I had jogged since then, and it felt great. After the jog, I stretched my muscles while taking in the sounds and sights of Saturday morning football being played on the oval next to my college.

In the space of those 24 hours after the EFT session, the depressive episode was comprehensively broken, and from there, life got a whole lot better.

Over the next several months, I consistently felt happy, not needing to sleep much and yet still having plenty of energy. My speech lost its anxiety-induced stutter, and the religious concepts that had been troubling me seemed to disappear.

As with so much that happened during this pre-diagnosis period, I would learn later that what I was experiencing was hypomania, which is characterised by an elevated and expansive mood, decreased need for sleep, increased energy, racing thoughts, impulsivity, and sometimes, reckless behaviour. It is a symptom of bipolar disorder, which is less severe than mania but can still disrupt daily functioning and cause problems in relationships or work.

For me, the period of hypomania was benign. It is good that I didn't have much money at my disposal because I made some impulsive decisions, such as signing up for a costly speed-reading short course with little practical benefit.

I also became enthused about unrealistic business ideas. I got as far as having introductory meetings with a few salespeople, which thankfully went nowhere in terms of me making financial commitments. It could have easily turned out differently.

Eventually, the hypomania fizzled out. In its place, the troubling religious thoughts came back. It was Easter of 2004, and I saw the newly released *The Passion of the Christ* at the cinema with some friends. It was a powerful and graphic film, and afterwards, I began thinking about Judas Iscariot and how the Gospel accounts portray his betrayal of Jesus. I started thinking about predestination and whether the Bible was saying that God wanted and planned for Judas to do what he did and whether Judas even had any choice in the matter.

Although I tried to move on and not think about it further, I simply couldn't. Soon, I was so preoccupied about it that I had to withdraw from my studies and move to live with my parents on the farm.

With the help of a different psychiatrist, we continued struggling to determine precisely what was wrong. Working on the farm seemed to make sense as an alternative to sitting around the house. Unfortunately, that year it involved handling sheep suffering from the effects of extreme drought.

Under the cumulative weight of three years of mental turmoil, this experience was a tipping point for me.

I started to believe I was a demon. It was *me* that was causing the drought and suffering around me.

Suicidal behaviours soon followed, and my mum, who was worried sick about me, picked up on these signals. My parents arranged for my hasty admission to the psychiatric hospital in Canberra where my new psychiatrist was a treating doctor. It was in the nick of time.

CHAPTER 2
A POSITIVE PSYCHIATRIC HOSPITAL EXPERIENCE

Let's pick up where I left off in the Introduction with my breakthrough experience with the mindfulness exercise in the hospital.

As that exercise showed me, I had been a captive to my thoughts. As the medication started to work, I needed strategies like the mindfulness exercise to bring these obsessive thoughts under control.

The second activity I learned to help break the obsessive thought cycle was "worry time", which involved dedicating a specific half hour in my day to focus my attention on thoughts that had been harassing me throughout the day and writing them down in a notebook.

The biggest challenge with deploying this exercise was the fear that in doing so, I was trivialising the seriousness of the thoughts which had preoccupied me for so long. Essentially, obsessive thoughts work by filling you with an unshakeable sense that those thoughts must take priority ahead of anything and everything else, as if your survival depends on it.

It felt like I was going against my conscience when I decided to try the worry time exercise for the first time, but I had been gaining confidence in knowing where my mental illness had been interfering with my good sense. The exercise turned out to be another excellent circuit breaker for my mind by giving me permission to avoid obsessing over the thoughts for the other 23.5 hours of the day.

Within a matter of days, the mindfulness and worry time exercises helped me get out of the mental zone I had been in for several months, where I was entirely preoccupied with my thoughts.

In the Introduction, I mentioned three aspects of my hospital treatment: medication, group and individual therapy, and the care and company of others. These deserve further explanation so you can see how they helped reset my mental state and direct my mental energy in the right direction.

Medication

I was put on lithium carbonate to treat the bipolar, and a tricyclic antidepressant known to counteract obsessive thoughts in addition to its mood-assisting qualities. Thankfully, this combination was a perfect fit for me, as the ensuing weeks would show. My condition improved via the reduction of obsessive thoughts, and my mood regained some stability. Over this time, my doctor adjusted the dosages with precision and was good at explaining what she was doing.

I was helped by a short book about lithium from the hospital's collection that served as a library for inpatients. The book explained the medication's intended role for people with bipolar disorder and gave me confidence that it might work for me. I still chuckle when I think about how often the word "prophylactic" (which means preventative) was used in the book, a term I had never heard before—clearly a book written by a doctor.

I highly recommend anyone experiencing mental illness educate themselves about the medications they have been prescribed. Many of the side effect troubles I experienced in my pre-diagnosis phase (during which time I was prescribed a series of powerful drugs) may have been avoided if I had known how important it was to do this.

Group and individual therapy

During the day, psychologists, social workers or nurses ran group therapy sessions. Over the course of a given week, they covered topics such as distress tolerance, art therapy, anger management, breathing exercises, and mindfulness.

There was a daily morning walk after breakfast and a weekly trip somewhere off the hospital campus. While none of the sessions or outings were compulsory, I was encouraged to attend them and did so to my great benefit. They all helped me to cope and recover, as well as get to know other inpatients and learn from them as well.

I saw my doctor twice a week to discuss how I was doing, did the same with my assigned psychologist or social worker, and had conversations of varying lengths with the nurses assigned to me daily.

Features of the hospital, such as its picturesque and quiet geographic location, the decor and size of my room, and the quality of the food, all contributed to a positive atmosphere for my recovery. In my subsequent work inspecting hospitals as a patient advocate, I have come to learn how fortunate I was compared with patients in most psychiatric hospitals, which are not nearly so well set up and lack structure to the day for inpatients with minimal opportunities for group therapy.

The care and company of others

During my time as a healthcare journalist (several years after my hospital experience), I interviewed Fred Lee, an American hospital executive whose insights into the importance of empathy and compassion in hospitals led him to author the bestselling book *If Disney Ran Your Hospital: 9 and a half things your hospital would do differently.*

Fred told me, "Psychoneuroimmunology is the study of the effect of people's thoughts on their nervous and immune systems, and there is plenty of this research to demonstrate that people who perceive genuine concern from those caring for them get better faster, and thus have shorter stays in hospital."

This insight matches up entirely with my experience. As an inpatient, I appreciated the patience and empathy of the many clinical and administrative staff members during my stay. The company of other people admitted for treatment was also a real highlight. I can vividly recall moments of camaraderie that still give me a warm glow when I think about them.

One such moment was a discussion I had over coffee with a fellow inpatient in one of the cafes on the hospital campus. There was an asymmetry to his face because he had cancer removed from his jawline, and he had subsequently been battling anxiety issues for several years. He had a gentle nature and a lisp because of the jaw operation.

It felt like we could have been two people in any city or town chatting things over. I remember it so well because, at the time, feeling "normal" was a fleeting sensation. The accumulation of little moments like this led to me gaining confidence in myself again.

The visits I received from family and friends were vital to my recovery, and the memories I have of these are powerful and fill me with deep joy and gratitude. I remember my mum bringing the most remarkable array of water lilies on my birthday (which happened to be the day after my admission to the hospital). They meant so much to me.

But I couldn't stay in the hospital forever. Once I had regained a decent level of mental stability, it was time to be discharged and begin the next phase of my recovery.

The Cold Harsh Light of Day

One of my favourite movies of all time is *A Beautiful Mind*, which tells the true story of Nobel Prize-winning mathematician John Nash. Without prior knowledge, viewers think that they are watching the dramatic story of a man working in top-secret intelligence who becomes entangled in the attempt to prevent Soviet forces from waging nuclear war on America.

Midway through the film, the viewers discover that what they had been watching was the world through the eyes of someone with psychosis that had not yet been detected. Up to that point in the film, the real and the imagined had been indistinguishable. It was apparent neither to Nash (played brilliantly by Russell Crowe) nor to the audience that there was any distinction to be made.

As it did in my own story, the turning point of the film happens in a psychiatric hospital where Nash is told he has schizophrenia. In one of the movie's most poignant scenes, Alicia Nash tells her husband that, far from the world facing nuclear Armageddon, it is all in Nash's head.

It was a remarkably similar experience to mine, only in my case, the diagnosis was bipolar disorder.

Psychosis is a mental state where the affected person loses touch with reality, which can involve either sensory hallucinations (i.e., seeing or hearing things that are not really there) or delusions (e.g., believing oneself to have superpowers). In Nash's case, his psychosis featured hallucinations, whereas for me it was delusions.

In an interview with the American Psychological Association, Nash described his experience of the "cold harsh light of day" after being diagnosed, leaving hospital, and learning how to manage his day-to-day life from that point onwards.

After eight weeks of living anywhere, you get comfortable and used to your routine and surroundings, so for me, the cold harsh light of day is a good description of those early months after leaving the hospital. This is because I was re-orienting my mind and body to everyday life without the degree of support one has in hospital.

PART 2
THE BODY

Naturally, there is always going to be overlap when discussing the body, mind and spirit. None of these elements operate in isolation because they are integrated parts of every person.

When I talk about the body, I am referring to the physical person's head to toe, including of course the brain. Beyond medication, there is so much that can be done to improve the health and functioning of the brain, which I am about to discuss.

What I learned in the early months and years of my recovery is that half the battle of conditions like bipolar disorder is managing my mental and physical energy.

Nutrition, exercise, and sleep are essential factors for any person's physical and mental well-being. In the context of my mental illness, they played a crucial role in my recovery, and they continue their vital place in my life today.

In simple terms, nutrition provides the body with essential nutrients that are necessary for the brain to function correctly. A balanced diet that includes a variety of fruits, vegetables, whole grains, lean proteins and healthy fats can help to maintain brain health and reduce symptoms of mental illness.

Exercise is also vital for mental health. Regular physical activity can help to reduce symptoms of anxiety and depression, improve mood, and increase self-esteem. Exercise can also help regulate the body's stress response system, which can benefit someone experiencing elevated stress levels.

Sleep is critical for mental health, as it provides the body with the necessary time to rest and repair. Lack of sleep can lead to increased feelings of anxiety and depression, difficulty concentrating, and memory problems. Getting enough sleep is essential for a person's overall well-being and can help reduce mental illness symptoms.

It has been my experience that there is a remarkable difference in mental health outcomes between doing a decent job versus an excellent job of managing these three body basics. Let's take a deeper look at each.

CHAPTER 3
NUTRITION

You don't need us to tell you about the typical Western diet. You already know that it's high in calories, refined grains, and sugar; it's heavily processed; and it's low in fresh produce, especially vegetables. In contrast, a healthy, Mediterranean-style diet is high in fresh vegetables and fruits, nuts, good fats, and fish. It's low in ultra-processed foods and sugary drinks. And here is the scary fact - government data from the United States, Canada, New Zealand, and Australia show that at least 50 percent of what we now put in our mouths does not even qualify as food. It is ultra-processed "stuff". Stuff made from simple carbs (sugar), salt, trans fats, and chemicals like artificial colouring.

Food is defined as nutritious substances we consume for growth and to maintain life. There has not been a single study showing that the Western diet is good for our mental health.

> – Dr Julia Rucklidge and Dr Bonnie Kaplan, 'The Better Brain: How Nutrition Will Help You Overcome Anxiety, Depression, ADHD and Stress'

As a young adult, I was vaguely familiar with the principles of good nutrition from what I learned at school. However, as someone with a sweet tooth, I was not a very disciplined eater.

My first proper encounter with a nutrition-informed diet was when I needed to lose weight after fracturing my foot. I had unknowingly piled on pounds from the antipsychotic medication my first psychiatrist prescribed without giving me fair warning about this side effect.

It was the beginning of soccer season, and the captain of my residential college team wanted me to get in shape. With the help of his girlfriend, who was studying nutrition, he gave me several pointers about what I needed to change with my eating habits. He was also good at policing my choices at the college dining hall!

That experience, which saw my weight successfully come back down, showed me what was possible with the right nutrition guidance and motivation to follow a plan.

Fast forward from that experience to when I found myself back in Sydney about two years after my hospital stay; I needed to find a new psychiatrist. This was because my excellent Canberra-based one who diagnosed me while I was in hospital was now geographically too far away for me to continue seeing her.

I lucked on a good recommendation from my GP. After my new psychiatrist got up to speed on my mental state, he promptly referred me to a doctor who specialised in endocrinology. This doctor was able to assess me and recommend changes to my diet that put me on a path to better physical and (therefore) mental health.

Informed as I was by my foot fracture recovery experience several years earlier, I had a positive attitude to the dietary advice the doctor gave me. It motivated me to cut out some of the poor eating habits I had picked up, such as snacking on junk food late at night and not having enough protein in my diet.

I credit the resulting adjustments to my diet as a major factor in increasing my productive capacity, which enabled me to complete my university studies. From that point on, I was capable of working full-time again, thanks to my better body condition and sharper mind.

But my positive nutrition journey didn't stop there. A couple of years later, I had the blessing of dating a nutritionist and medical herbalist who is now my wife. The further improvements she was able to bring to my diet and the herbal supplements I now take are major factors in making it possible for me to be the healthy, full-time working dad I am today.

She has taught me the importance of gut health, a vital component of overall well-being, often referred to as the "second brain" due to its intricate neural network. Notably, 50 percent of dopamine and 90 percent of serotonin, key neurotransmitters influencing mood, are produced in the gut. This underscores the profound impact of gut health on mental and emotional states. Furthermore, our gut hosts a complex microbiome, housing 100 trillion microorganisms of 15,000 bacterial species. A balanced microbiome is essential for digestion, immune system function, and overall health. I have learned that maintaining gut health through a diverse diet, probiotics, and healthy habits is paramount, as it affects digestion, mental health, immunity, and overall well-being. In contrast, a compromised gut can lead to health issues and nutrient deficiencies.

For those not fortunate enough to marry one, I highly recommend consulting an expert in nutrition and natural health to see how they can optimise your health and well-being. With the advice you receive from experts, remember that you are in charge and need to find what works for you over the long term. There has been plenty of trial and error in finding what foods have been the best fit for me and the accommodations my body needs for things to be sustainable.

For example, I found that the lack of carbohydrates in the endocrinologist's recommendations for the evening meal left me cranky and irritable, as did his directive to not have anything sweet after the meal. Consequently, I built in things to address this so that I can enjoy my evenings (without overdoing it).

Here are my personal top six nutrition tips.

1. **Fresh food**: There is simply no substitute for beautiful, fresh, unprocessed food. Fresh, whole foods are rich in essential nutrients like vitamins, minerals, and antioxidants that support mental health. Antioxidants, found in colourful fruits and vegetables, help protect the brain from oxidative stress, reducing the risk of cognitive decline and mood disorders. Fresh foods also provide dietary fibre, which supports a healthy gut microbiome and promotes regularity.

2. **Protein**: Protein is an essential part of my diet and is something I did not properly appreciate as a young adult. Once I learned that protein takes longer to digest and helps me stay full long after having a meal, I have ensured it is part of every meal I have.

It helps to stabilise blood sugar levels, preventing the energy crashes and irritability often associated with sugar-laden foods. Including sources of lean protein in your diet, such as poultry, fish, and tofu, can help ensure a steady supply of neurotransmitters like serotonin and dopamine, which play pivotal roles in regulating mood and emotions. I am also a fan of red meat, which is an excellent source of protein and other nutrients such as iron, zinc, and B vitamins (B12, B6, niacin), which support muscle development, immune function, and red blood cell production. I try to stick to lean cuts of red meat to minimise my saturated fat intake.

3. **Slow-burning carbs**: Complex carbohydrates, found in foods like whole grains, legumes and vegetables provide a sustained release of energy, helping to stabilise blood sugar levels and curb cravings. This steady energy supply from foods with a low glycaemic index (GI) enhances mental alertness and supports physical endurance. I make sure slow-burning carbs are part of every meal I have, starting with breakfast, which, for me, is the most carb-heavy of my three daily meals. Additionally, slow-burning carbs are rich in fibre, promoting digestive health, and I have found they contribute to long-term weight control by promoting satiety and reducing overall calorie consumption. Incorporating these nutrient-dense foods into your diet can lead to improved energy levels, better weight management, and enhanced overall well-being.

4. **Good fats and oils**: It's important to know that not all fats are bad. Indeed, the healthy types such as omega-3 fatty acids found in certain kinds of fish (e.g., salmon), flaxseed, and walnuts have properties that can reduce inflammation in the brain, lowering the risk of depression and anxiety. These fats are integral to the structure of brain cells and are vital for cognitive function and mood regulation. Incorporating sources of healthy fats, like avocados, olive oil, almonds and cashews can support better

mental well-being. From a dairy perspective, I opt for full cream milk because it is rich in calcium, vitamin D, and protein, which support bone health, immune function and muscle growth, and helps me feel full. Regarding spreads, butter contains healthy fats such as omega-3 fatty acids and is far healthier than margarine, which typically contains nasty trans fats, inflammatory fats and synthetic additives.

5. **Healthy snacks**: Opting for nutrient-dense snacks over sugary or processed alternatives has had a profound impact on my mood stability. Nutrient-rich snacks provide sustained energy without the spikes and crashes associated with sugary snacks. Regular snacking on items like yoghurt with berries, mixed nuts, or carrot sticks with hummus helps maintain stable blood sugar levels, reducing mood swings and irritability throughout the day. I recommend reading the ingredients on the label when buying snacks. For instance, when purchasing nut bars, I choose one with the highest proportion of nuts and the smallest amounts of sugar and other additives.

6. **Timing**: Being deliberate about the timing of meals and spacing out when I eat snacks has been important for maintaining stable energy levels. Eating balanced meals and snacks at regular intervals helps regulate blood sugar, preventing energy slumps that can lead to irritability and low mood. How this looks will differ from person to person, but I am an advocate for having three square meals a day and making sure I sit down for them, chew properly and mindfully enjoy them so that my brain and body feel connected. Having a hearty breakfast gets me through to lunch with minimal snacking, but I need snacks to manage the interval between lunch and dinner. But as I say, it's a personal thing, so make sure you optimise how you manage timing with meals and snacks so that it works to your benefit.

Incorporating these practices into my daily eating habits has improved my mental well-being by providing the necessary nutrients for mood stability and brain health. Keep in mind that personalised dietary choices may vary, and consulting with a healthcare professional can provide tailored guidance for your specific needs.

Nutrient therapy

One of the biggest secrets to my success has been something that my wife (a health practitioner) advised me to do: see an Integrative GP who specialises in nutrient therapy and who can compound nutritional medicines at appropriate doses for the individual.

Nutrient therapy is based on the generally accepted premise that most mental disorders involve imbalanced levels of critically important brain chemicals called neurotransmitters.

In simple terms, what the therapy involves is the diagnosis of a patient's nutrient imbalances through the testing of blood and urine. The treating doctor then prescribes nutrients in the form of vitamins, minerals, and other natural biochemicals to normalise the imbalances.

In my case, the prescription was filled by a compounding pharmacy, which dispensed the supplement regime to me in pill capsules. I have taken them morning and night ever since, complete with periodic check-ins with the GP and tests to see how my biochemistry is going.

In the book *Nutrient Power: Heal Your Biochemistry and Heal Your Brain*, Dr William Walsh notes, "A major advantage of biochemical therapy is the absence of the serious side effects associated with psychiatric medications. This medical approach uses natural chemicals rather than molecules that are foreign to the brain and induce an abnormal condition. Biochemical therapy can be used together with medication and counseling, providing great flexibility to the mental health practitioner."

Here is the fascinating part: although my psychiatrist was a believer in the importance of diet for good mental health, he told me this entire nutrient therapy exercise would be a waste of time (but not harmful, in his opinion). Nutrient therapy has not yet been widely accepted by the medical profession.

However, my experience has been that ever since I started taking the supplements, my mental and physical health has improved to a whole new level. I am much sharper mentally, can concentrate for longer, experience less drowsiness, and can manage on less sleep if, for whatever reason, it's not a great night (which, as a parent of young children, happens often enough).

I must emphasise that this therapy is not a replacement for medication and is not something you should experiment with by yourself. Just like with other prescriptions, the medical practitioner makes their assessment based on understanding the person's medical history, traits, and symptoms.

Personally, I swear by nutrient therapy for my health. It is well worth seeking advice from your healthcare practitioner on whether this is something they think may assist you.

CHAPTER 4
EXERCISE

Our bodies are pretty amazing and our brain, in particular, is a magical, wonderful tool. But if something goes wrong you can be seriously derailed and it can be hard to recalibrate. When someone has a form of depression - in whatever form that takes (eating disorders, self-harm etc) - it is all about hurting. It's about having an issue to deal with and that is never the same for everyone.

I truly believe that the key to long-term mental and physical health is intervention - not with medication unless medical intervention is a last resort, but moving and fuelling your body properly so that you don't have to try to avoid that dark place to begin with. We shouldn't wait until something terrible happens and then try to cure it, we should have the tools to nurture and take care of ourselves rather than relying on pills. Our bodies and minds are finely tuned machines and need careful feeding and maintaining. It isn't just about eating good food and getting fit, it is also about how you use fitness and nutrition as a way of feeling good and being better than you think you can be.

> – Kelly Holmes, 'Running Life: Mindset, fitness & nutrition for positive wellbeing'

The words above by Olympic gold medallist Kelly Holmes, who herself experienced depression, resonate deeply with me.

Although I was someone who did regular exercise throughout my school years via team sports, as a young adult, I was not conscious of its importance for my mental health.

Consequently, during my pre-diagnosis rollercoaster years, when it wasn't basketball or soccer season, I did not exercise much. When I look back, I can see it was no coincidence that my deepest depressive troughs were during the sporting off-seasons.

Not long after I was discharged from the hospital, my mum recommended I have weekly sessions with a personal trainer. It was a new experience for me, and immediately, it had a positive impact on my well-being. The trainer was good at explaining the different exercises and which muscles they were working on. She put together a plan for the exercises she recommended that I do on my own time.

Like the expert advice I received on nutrition, I credit the personal trainer's work with helping me achieve a marked improvement in my mental health.

I joined the university gym when I returned to Sydney to resume my studies. I decided I would try managing my exercise routine on my own without the assistance of a personal trainer and soon found that group fitness classes were a good fit for me when I wasn't playing team sports. The classes took place in large studios at the gym where a qualified trainer instructed groups of people in 30, 45 or 60-minute blocks with the exercises choreographed to music. A wide variety of classes were offered that catered to different personal tastes. I found being in that setting, alongside others and under instruction, worked well to motivate me to have a good workout.

The beauty of moderate to intense physical exercise is that it generates endorphins, which are neurotransmitters that act as natural painkillers and mood enhancers. During exercise, endorphins are released by the pituitary gland and the hypothalamus in the brain, and they bind to opiate receptors, similar to the way that opioids like morphine and heroin do.

Endorphins can benefit mental health in several ways. First, they can produce a sense of euphoria and well-being, which can help reduce symptoms of anxiety and depression. Second, endorphins can help reduce the perception of pain and discomfort, which can help improve mood and increase motivation to continue exercising. Third, endorphins can help regulate appetite and sleep, which are key factors in maintaining overall mental health.

Studies have shown that regular exercise can increase endorphin levels in the brain, leading to long-term improvements in mental health. For example, exercise has been shown to reduce symptoms of depression, anxiety and stress, and it can improve cognitive function and overall mood. Additionally, regular exercise has been linked to improvements in self-esteem and body image, which can help to boost overall mental health and well-being.

An important thing to note about exercise is that all movement counts, not just the intense stuff when we have our activewear on. For instance, the walking you already do (e.g., to the shops, to the bus stop) or additional walking you build into the day (e.g., 10-15 minutes during your lunch break) is valuable. I know people who try to do 10,000 steps a day and have a smartwatch or other device that helps them keep track of this.

Resistance training (strength training) is an essential complement to cardiovascular exercise. It can be as simple as using a pair of dumbbells or bodyweight resistance exercises such as push-ups, sit-ups and squats. The beauty of adding resistance training to your routine is that it increases several important things: muscle mass, bone density, metabolism rate, calorie burn and heart and blood flow. Consequently, it is widely recognised to positively impact mental health.

As with nutrition, trial and error is necessary to find which exercise routine works best for you. Plus, your taste, interests and circumstances can change over time, leading to the need to explore different options.

Like most others, when the Covid-19 pandemic hit in 2020, I had to live without access to the gym, and I adapted by doing much more outdoor running and self-guided body weight resistance training. Even now, with gyms back to proper operation, the stage I am currently at with raising our young children means that I am still in the gym-less exercise routine I started during the pandemic. The lesson here is that what works can change over time, and that's fine. What matters is ensuring exercise remains a priority so you can keep those endorphins flowing.

Keep in mind that these days, there are a great many online resources such as fitness apps and personal training YouTube channels that can help you exercise by yourself cheaply and effectively, so don't let money be an excuse for not exercising more.

CHAPTER 5
SLEEP

More than a third of adults in many developed nations fail to obtain the recommended seven to nine hours of nightly sleep.

I doubt you are surprised by this fact, but you may be surprised by the consequences. Routinely sleeping less than six hours a night weakens your immune system, substantially increasing your risk of certain forms of cancer. Insufficient sleep appears to be a key lifestyle factor linked to your risk of developing Alzheimer's disease. Inadequate sleep—even moderate reductions for just one week—disrupts blood sugar levels so profoundly that you would be classified as pre-diabetic. Short sleeping increases the likelihood of your coronary arteries becoming blocked and brittle, setting you on a path toward cardiovascular disease, stroke, and congestive heart failure. Fitting Charlotte Brontë's prophetic wisdom that 'a ruffled mind makes a restless pillow,' sleep disruption further contributes to all major psychiatric conditions, including depression, anxiety, and suicidality.

–   Matthew Walker, 'Why We Sleep: The New Science of Sleep and Dreams'

The last but not least of my three body basics is sleep.

As evidenced in the quote above from Matthew Walker's bestselling book, there has been a trove of sleep research in the last 25 years that has really advanced our knowledge of this essential part of life.

Adequate sleep is crucial to a person's physical and mental health. Sleep is the natural process that allows the body and brain to rest and repair, and it plays a vital role in maintaining good health.

Physically, sleep is essential for a healthy immune system, proper hormone regulation, and optimal metabolism. During sleep, the body produces cytokines, a protein that helps fight off infections and inflammation. Lack of sleep has been linked to an increased risk of developing chronic conditions such as obesity, diabetes, cardiovascular disease, and even cancer.

Sleep is crucial for cognitive function, emotional regulation and overall mental health. It helps consolidate memories and learning, and a lack of sleep has been linked to poor decision-making, decreased attention and concentration, and an increased risk of developing mental health conditions such as anxiety and depression.

Furthermore, sleep is essential for regulating mood and emotional well-being. Lack of sleep can lead to irritability, mood swings, and decreased tolerance for stress, which can further exacerbate mental health conditions.

A healthy sleep routine that allows for enough restorative sleep can help boost the immune system, regulate hormones, improve cognitive function, regulate emotions, and reduce the risk of developing chronic conditions and mental health issues.

Anyone with a mental illness has difficulty at times with their sleep, and I am no exception. One of the ways I made myself susceptible to the mental breakdown that kicked off with the 9/11 attacks was the shortage of sleep I had during the preceding two-year period (2000-2001). In my final year of school (in 2000), I would often study late into the night and be up early as per the morning routine of the boarding school. My sleep shortage in 2001 was just as dire since I was cramming in full-time work and part-time study, which again meant late nights and even earlier mornings.

I described earlier how being prescribed an antipsychotic before I was diagnosed correctly caused me to eat much more than usual, and the other thing it did was lead to me oversleeping due to its powerful sedative qualities. Such was its potency that I would often sleep well into the late morning and even early afternoon, which was far more than my body needed.

Conversely, during my hypomanic phase, I was so full of energy that I was happily operating on about four or five hours of sleep for those several months.

In the months leading up to my hospital admission in 2004, the severe depression massively interrupted my sleep, and it was only after I was diagnosed and put on the right medication that my sleep finally normalised after what had been a problematic few years.

I say that my sleep normalised, but my post-diagnosis journey with sleep has nevertheless had its ups and downs. One of the most challenging times I have had since then was about 10 years ago when I convinced my psychiatrist to let me try coming off my antidepressant (while staying on my mood stabiliser).

Initially, it seemed to go well, and the increased emotional range I enjoyed as a result felt fantastic. Before long, however, I was having trouble with my sleep. It took a couple of months for us to figure out that I was suffering from restless legs syndrome, which was causing insomnia. It turned out that the restless legs were a side effect of the mood stabiliser, which only revealed itself after I came off the antidepressant, which had been masking that side effect.

During that time, I was only able to get about four or five hours of sleep per night. Physically, I felt terrible, and managing work was so difficult that I needed to drop to four days a week. Once the problem was identified, it took another several months to get the medication levels right again and for my sleep to normalise.

The following are my hard-won insights into what I do (and what I avoid) in order to enjoy quality and adequate sleep.

An important thing for me is having good "sleep hygiene". This refers to a set of practices and habits that can help promote quality sleep and prevent sleep disturbances. It includes various behavioural and environmental factors that can affect one's ability to fall asleep and stay asleep.

The three main aspects of my sleep hygiene are having a consistent sleep schedule, creating a sleep-conducive environment, and limiting screen time before bed.

I have found that maintaining a consistent sleep schedule helps to regulate my body's internal clock and promotes better sleep quality. Best practice is to go to bed and wake up at the same time every day, even on weekends. I bend the rules a little with this on weekends and on the days I need to wake up earlier to commute to work (I mainly work from home), but not by much.

Creating a sleep-conducive environment involves making sure my bedroom is primarily used for sleep and distinct from the areas of my home where I do after-dinner activities such as watching TV. Some find it helpful to use blackout curtains or eye masks to block out any light and earplugs or white noise to mask any unwanted noise.

Limiting screen use before attempting sleep is one of the most important steps I take. The blue light emitted from electronic devices such as smartphones, tablets, and computers can suppress the production of the melatonin hormone and interfere with your ability to fall asleep. This is especially the case with social media platforms' bright white screens, which I consider a definite no-no in bed or directly beforehand. It is recommended to avoid using electronic devices for at least an hour before bedtime. Ever since I began following the one-hour-before-bed rule, the quality of my sleep has improved enormously.

When reading books at bedtime, for several years now I have used an eReader so that I don't need a lamp to light the page, which disturbed my wife, who tends to go to sleep before I do. The eReader allows me to read in the dark without having the stimulating blue light effect of smartphones and other electronic devices.

As you can see from my experience, life can throw curve balls at someone with a mental illness when it comes to getting a good night's sleep. As with nutrition and exercise, being deliberate about optimising your sleep is worth the investment of your time and energy, complete with the necessary trial and error.

CHAPTER 6
MEDICATION AND SIDE EFFECTS

As you have seen from my own experience, medication has been essential to my recovery and ongoing wellness. Unfortunately, side effects can be a major source of difficulty for people on medication to live with.

The first step to addressing the challenges associated with medication side effects is to educate oneself about what you have been prescribed. I had the misfortune during my pre-diagnosis phase of having a psychiatrist who did not explain to me the potential side effects of what he was prescribing. Had I been aware of the importance of understanding side effects, I would have asked him questions each time he prescribed me something new.

In addition to asking one's doctor, all medications require a pamphlet with information about potential side effects, and that is always a good thing to read. Asking a pharmacist about side effects when buying your prescribed medication is also a good idea since they are trained to assist people with questions about side effects.

Drowsiness and constipation are two medication side effects that have been part of my experience and are pretty common to a lot of medications used to treat mental illness.

Drowsiness

In the first few years of being on antidepressants and mood stabilisers, every day I felt drowsy for the first few hours after waking. It was not a fun experience.

This meant that getting out of bed was a challenge because of the tiredness I felt upon waking. In settings where I was sitting and listening to someone speaking, such as morning lectures at university or in church, staying awake was a genuine battle.

One way to reduce drowsiness is to adjust the timing of medication. For example, taking medication at night before bedtime can help minimise the impact of drowsiness during the day. I found that I needed to tinker with the timing of when to take medication, along with when to go to bed and when to wake up. Like I have said with other things, trial and error is necessary and worth the effort.

Over time, the better I have managed diet, exercise, and sleep, the better my experience with drowsiness has been.

Alcohol, caffeine and sugar are three substances to watch out for since they can exacerbate drowsiness caused by medication.

Indeed, one of the medications I take has a warning in large writing: "This medicine may cause drowsiness and may increase the effects of alcohol. If affected, do not drive a motor vehicle or operate heavy machinery." I actually avoid alcohol completely since it has never agreed with my body anyway, but if that is not you, just make sure you speak with your healthcare professional about it and are aware of alcohol's compounding effect.

Caffeine is a stimulant that can increase alertness and reduce feelings of fatigue and is thus a consideration for helping people live with the sedative effect of certain medications. However, it can also interfere with the body's natural sleep-wake cycle, making it harder to fall asleep and stay asleep. This can lead to further sleep disturbances, which can exacerbate the drowsiness caused by medication.

Furthermore, some medications can interact with caffeine and cause adverse effects. For example, caffeine can interact with certain antidepressants, causing nervousness, restlessness, and an increased heart rate. In addition, caffeine can increase blood pressure and heart rate, which can be dangerous for people with certain medical conditions.

In my case, I have found that I feel too restless and do not think very clearly if I drink coffee, but a cup of English breakfast tea in the morning helps to wake me up and doesn't give me any adverse effects. If I have that same cup of tea in the afternoon, however, it keeps me up at night.

Sugar is something else to watch out for. Consuming sugar can lead to a rapid increase in blood glucose levels, which can cause a corresponding increase in insulin levels to manage the blood sugar. The sudden drop in blood sugar levels can cause feelings of drowsiness and fatigue, particularly in people who are already experiencing drowsiness as a side effect of medication for a mental illness.

In my case, a natural affinity for sweet things meant that my consumption of sugar, while not particularly high compared with the general population, was still a contributing factor in making my drowsiness more difficult than it needed to be.

This is where the work I did (with healthcare professional guidance) on improving my nutrition and eating habits paid dividends. I now eat a balanced diet with low glycemic index foods, avoid sugary drinks and am wary about snacking on foods with added sugars. This has helped me maintain stable blood sugar levels throughout the day and reduced the severity of drowsiness as a side effect of medication.

The last thing I will say about drowsiness is that if you feel it is making life too difficult, talk to your doctor about lowering the dosage or changing the medication. They can work with you to find a medication that is effective in treating your condition while minimising unwanted side effects.

Constipation

Anyone who has experienced constipation can attest to the bugbear it can be to their quality of life. The physical discomfort and pain associated with constipation can lead to feelings of irritability, frustration and embarrassment. It can disrupt a person's sleep patterns and contribute to fatigue and difficulty concentrating, which can further exacerbate depression and anxiety.

Owing to the high dosage of the antidepressant I was on after being diagnosed in hospital, constipation was a side effect I had to deal with early on in my recovery journey. Although these days I am on a lower dose of that drug, it is something that would still be an issue for me had I not learned ways to prevent it from being a problem.

Having a diet high in fibre helps to promote regular bowel movements by adding bulk to stools and stimulating the muscles in the digestive system. Foods like fruits, vegetables, whole grains, and legumes are excellent sources of fibre. Thanks to my wife's naturopathic guidance, I also swear by flaxseed meal, which I sprinkle on my breakfast, and dandelion tea, which I have in the afternoon and evening which aids in good digestive health and regularity.

Being on lithium reduced the amount of water that my body was absorbing in the colon, and thus teamed up with the antidepressant to cause constipation when I was first diagnosed. Through this experience, I learned the importance of adequate hydration. Drinking enough water is essential for maintaining good digestive health, helping to soften stools, making them easier to pass. Even though it has now been years since I was on lithium, the good water-drinking habits I developed during that time have stayed with me.

Regular exercise can help stimulate the muscles in the digestive tract, which can promote regular bowel movements. Even a moderate amount of exercise, such as brisk walking, can be beneficial for digestive health. Getting moving is one of the best things you can do to help get things moving inside your body.

I should also mention probiotics, which are beneficial bacteria that live in the gut and can help improve digestive health. Incorporating probiotic-rich foods like yoghurt and kefir into the diet can help promote regularity, as can probiotic supplements. They have certainly helped me and are part of my daily consumption.

In summary, a well-balanced diet that is high in fibre, adequate hydration, regular exercise, and the incorporation of probiotics can all help counter constipation and promote good digestive health.

PART 3
THE MIND

Now that we have examined how to look after the body and optimise it to support your mental health, let's turn to matters of the mind. Like I said in the Introduction, how you think goes a long way in determining how mentally healthy you are.

If, like me, you have hospital grade mental health issues, then the guidance of healthcare professionals is going to be essential to working things through. In this part of the book, I will discuss the key learnings from my many years of therapy and what have been the most practical insights into improving and strengthening my mindset to make it resilient during life's inevitable ups and downs.

Although depression and anxiety often overlap, I address them separately in this part of the book to highlight the specific strategies that have helped me manage and overcome each of these conditions.

CHAPTER 7
SIX STRATEGIES TO COUNTER DEPRESSION

One of my all-time favourite documentary shows is *Air Crash Investigations*. Each episode recounts a plane crash and tells the story of the investigation into what happened and why. Time and again, the investigators conclude that it is rarely a single problem that causes an air disaster, but rather a combination or "cascade" of factors.

The same can be said for falling into depression. Lots of seemingly little things can contribute to a personal emotional crash. The good news is that minor adjustments to how you direct your mental energy can go a long way to preventing a nosedive or help with pulling out of one. I use six rules of thumb to help keep myself level when things are difficult.

1. Reframing

Reframing is a technique used in therapy that involves changing the way a person thinks about a situation in order to change their emotional response to it. For a person with depression, reframing can be a helpful tool to challenge negative thoughts and beliefs that contribute to their low mood.

One way to reframe negative thoughts is to identify and challenge cognitive distortions, which are irrational or unhelpful ways of thinking that can contribute to depression. Examples of cognitive distortions include all-or-nothing thinking, overgeneralisation, and emotional reasoning.

One of the best books I have read about improving one's state of mind is *Your Brain at Work* by David Rock, which has an excellent chapter about reframing (which he refers to as reappraisal). "Kevin Ochsner, at Columbia University, studies the neuroscience of reappraisal… 'There's a famous finding in the psychological literature,' Ochsner explains, 'showing that six months later, someone who has become a paraplegic is just as happy as someone who's won the lottery. It seems clear people are doing something to find what's positive in even the direst of circumstances. The one thing you can always do is control your interpretation of the meaning of the situation, and that's fundamentally what reappraisal is all about.'"

A therapist can work with a person with depression to identify and challenge their negative thinking patterns and help them develop more adaptive and realistic ways of thinking about themselves and their situation. Additionally, practising reframing regularly can help build resilience and reduce the impact of negative thoughts on mood.

I have found that, in my experience, reframing soon becomes a habit once you know how to identify and challenge the interpretations causing you to feel depressed. Before long, it becomes second nature.

2. Make expectations your friend rather than your enemy

I think of managing expectations as the sister to reframing because it is also about changing the way you think, and it can be just as life-changing.

In *Your Brain At Work*, David Rock discusses the work of Professor Wolfram Schultz from Cambridge University, who is an expert on the links between dopamine and the reward circuitry of the brain. "Schultz found that when a cue from the environment indicates you're going to get a reward, dopamine is released in response. Unexpected rewards release more dopamine than expected ones. Thus, the surprise bonus at work, even a small one, can positively impact your brain chemistry more than an expected pay raise. However, if you're expecting a reward and you don't get it, dopamine levels fall steeply. This feeling is not a pleasant one; it feels a lot like pain." Rock refers to other research that indicates "the right dose of expectations can be as powerful as one of the strongest painkillers."

Clearly, expectations are powerful things, and you can make them either work for you or against you. During my recovery, as I became more mindful of how my brain was operating and learning to correct problematic thinking, unrealistic expectations were an area that required plenty of correction. A lot of this was about tempering my expectations of best-case scenarios that are so often not met.

An object example is watching my favourite rugby league team play. As I watch the match, I am hoping that my beloved Canberra Raiders will defeat the team they are playing. If I am not careful, that hope becomes an expectation, which sets me up for disappointment about 50 percent of the time when the Raiders do not win. So, instead, I have learned to put that hope in perspective by saying to myself: "Yes, I hope they win, but in sport, you win some and you lose some, and both outcomes are just as likely. I want to enjoy watching the game and just let it happen." I find it also helps to add the bigger picture perspective that sport is a fun activity and not life or death. Ultimately, it is just a game of sport.

This might seem like a trivial example, but when problematic expectations are multiplied across all aspects of one's life, they can accumulate and have a powerful depressive effect.

So be realistic. It is natural for best-case scenarios to dominate expectations for the routine aspects of life. Average-case scenarios are a much better guide.

3. Identify the spikes

Seeing the bigger picture is important for all of us, especially if we are under stress and tend to be anxious or glum. Think of any given period in your life, whether a day, week, month or year. If you were to plot your feelings on a graph, there would likely be primarily shallow waves, a few highs, and a few downward spikes of distress. How we handle these spikes can greatly affect how things play out.

This is where the practice of mindfulness comes into its own. I found that it did not take long for it to permeate my state of mind, making me far more conscious of what was going on with my brain and body. Half the battle is won once I recognise that I am in a spike of distress. At that point, I can make decisions about how things play out rather than simply letting my emotions run riot.

Dr. Dan Siegel's Hand Model of the Brain is a simple yet powerful tool that has helped me understand the neurobiology of emotions and how to regulate them effectively. Siegel uses the hand as a metaphor to explain the various parts of the brain and their functions. Imagine your palm as the brainstem (reptilian brain, basic functions), the thumb as the limbic regions (mid brain), and your fingers as the cerebral cortex (upper brain, logic centre). When you make a fist by curling your fingers over your thumb, it represents the brain working in harmony, with each part of the brain communicating effectively.

On his YouTube channel, Siegel says the key to emotional regulation is to prevent your "flipped lid". In the Hand Model, this is where the fingers lose contact with the thumb and stretch out, which represents the moment when your prefrontal cortex is overwhelmed and quits effectively communicating with the limbic system. When your lid flips, you may act impulsively, say things you don't mean, or engage in behaviour you later regret.

To maintain control over your emotions and prevent the lid from flipping, Siegel suggests using mindfulness techniques. By practising mindfulness, you can observe your negative feelings as they arise, acknowledge them, and create space between the trigger and your response.

When you pause to recognise your emotions, you allow your prefrontal cortex to come back online and help regulate your reactions more effectively. This way, you can respond to challenging situations with greater emotional intelligence and make more thoughtful choices.

4. This too shall pass

One of the most important insights I can share about handling depression is that how you feel at a given point in time is not a permanent state. Depression has an inherently deceptive quality that tells the sufferer: "How you are feeling now is inescapably permanent, and nothing you can do is going to change that."

The good news is that nothing could be further from the truth. Abraham Lincoln once said:

> An Eastern monarch once charged his wise men to invent him a sentence, to be ever in view, and which should be true and appropriate in all times and situations. They presented him the words: 'And this, too, shall pass away.' How much it

expresses! How chastening in the hour of pride! How consoling in the depths of affliction! 'And this, too, shall pass away.'

As a child, Lincoln had very few books available to read. His stepmother said Lincoln sought to learn and understand every detail of the texts. She said that when something was "fixed in his mind to suit him, he never lost that fact or the understanding of it." It may require some repeating to get through to yourself that "this, too, shall pass." It certainly took a while for me. It remains one of the most valuable truths I have ever learned.

5. Accept what you cannot change

Over the years, I have wasted a ton of mental energy thinking about something in the past that I wish I could change, or some ongoing reality over which I have no control. I am talking about more than simply wishing something were not so. I mean the stewing or brooding that perpetuates negative emotions like fear or anger. These thoughts and feelings pull me away from the present moment and prevent me from acknowledging that there is nothing I can do about the memory or circumstance, and therefore keep me from being able to move on.

A prayer attributed to Saint Francis of Assisi says, "God grant me the serenity to accept the things I cannot change, the courage to change the things I can, and the wisdom to know the difference between the two."

I appreciate that this is much easier said than done, especially when it comes to life-changing events or developments that lead to hardship or heartbreak. Nevertheless, the sooner we come to grips with our circumstances and consciously acknowledge that we cannot change the past, the sooner we can focus on how to proceed healthily with positive motivation.

6. Things aren't always as they seem

As someone who has experienced psychosis, you could say I have strong testimony to back up the statement that things aren't always as they seem. But you don't need to have been healed from psychosis to embed this truth into your own life and keep it in the front of your mind when the chips are down.

At the outset of the 2015-2016 season, bookmakers gave odds of 5000/1 for the Leicester City Football Club to win the English Premier League. They were a team that had narrowly escaped relegation the previous year, barely avoiding demotion to a lower division. In short, to everyone outside the coach and players, they were losers heading for another season of losing. But that's not what happened.

Leicester City's eventual victory in that Premier League season is etched in sporting history as a testament to what is possible, not just in sports but also in life. In the face of daunting odds, unwavering belief combined with positive action can transform what seems impossible into reality.

The application point of this story is simple: things are not always as they seem. You might feel like the odds of recovering from depression and regaining your mental health and well-being are 5000/1, but I can tell you from experience that it's just the depression saying that. The truth is, with persistence, you can and will recover.

CHAPTER 8
SIX STRATEGIES TO COUNTER ANXIETY

As I have already shared, anxiety first affected my life when I was in my late teens. I worked full-time, attended university at night, and studied on weekends. I remember operating at a frantic pace and feeling frustrated at my lack of time for many things I wanted to do, such as meeting up with friends and exercising.

I didn't realise at the time how vulnerable I was, leaving myself susceptible to mental deterioration, and before long, I began experiencing panic attacks and episodes of depression.

In my case, a major incident caused me to stop and think about how sustainably I was living. I advocate not waiting for one of these.

It was during my stay in hospital in 2004 that I began to win the battle with anxiety through practices such as the mindfulness exercise.

It is fair to say that no one with a history of anxiety can say they are 100 percent cured—much like what they teach at Alcoholics Anonymous. The principles I learned in hospital remain highly relevant to my ongoing health and well-being management, and I have built on these principles over the years.

One of my favourite quotes of all time is from the TV drama *The Wire*. A senior and a junior detective (Lester and Prez) are surveilling a drug dealer's phone calls (let's leave aside the ethics of this for another time). Prez is tasked with recording which conversations are pertinent and which ones are not. After a while, he tires of the task and expresses his frustration.

Lester looks over the glasses resting on his nose and says to his junior, "We're building a case, detective, and all the pieces matter."

So it is with managing anxiety. We add a piece to our wellness whenever we avoid a mistake that beset us yesterday. All the pieces matter.

Here are my most frequently deployed strategies for containing anxiety.

1. Regulate your speed

A key aspect of my anxiety issues has been the tendency to rush just about anything I do. Of course, there can be good reasons to rush. If I am at an airport and need to make a connecting flight, I will happily concede feeling light-headed from the dash once I am on the plane.

Furthermore, our reasons for hurrying are often noble. Perhaps you are a conscientious worker motivated by the desire to do a good job. Or maybe you want to get through what you are doing so you can get home in time to read your daughter a bedtime story.

We are often keenly aware of the positives associated with hurrying but less so with the negatives. It has been my experience that rushing almost always has a negative payoff, and often, we do not factor it into our decision-making.

To illustrate the negative payoff by hurrying, we can apply the concept of inertia to how the mind works. I first learned about inertia at school, watching crash-test dummies being propelled through car windshields. The principle of inertia is that objects moving at speed have momentum. The person operating at an unsustainably fast mental speed creates their own kind of inertia, which affects that person long after they have decided to stop whatever it was that they were doing.

For me, "hurry inertia" (as I call it) has involved an ugly emotional mixture of guilt, instability and a lack of confidence in myself that I cannot seem to place nor easily shrug off. These feelings are then compounded by the fact that in my hurried state, I become less considerate of others and am prone to poor decision-making.

It is easy to become overly busy without consciously realising the danger to your mental health. You may even complain to your friends, family and work colleagues for months or even years without realising inwardly what you have been telling them.

Allow things to take the time they are supposed to—don't let something you would ordinarily enjoy become arduous by being rushed. For example,

I have found myself feeling far less anxious since I began stopping properly for meals.

As with so many aspects of mental health, the key point I want to make here is awareness. Resolve to be more aware of the speed at which you operate. This will open new possibilities in your day-to-day life and result in a healthier you.

2. FOMO is a no-no

In the months after I was discharged from the hospital and was convalescing at home, I had no employment or study requirements to fulfil and no obligations to volunteer my time anywhere. Yet inexplicably, my sense of anxiety over not having enough time was as acute as it had ever been.

I believe this anxiety had its roots in earlier periods where I had overloaded myself and was overwhelmed with frustration about the things I was missing out on.

A fundamental belief underlying this anxiety about "fear of missing out" (FOMO in today's parlance) is that life's blessings are scarce and related to time constraints.

This experience taught me a valuable lesson I try these days not to forget: feeling as if you don't have the time to do what you need to do promotes anxiety. Additionally, it goes against good mental health to be constantly kept from at least some of the things you would like to do.

Banjo Paterson, one of Australia's best-known poets, had this in mind when he penned one of his most famous works, *Clancy of the Overflow*. He describes the fast-paced nature of city life in the 1880s (I wonder what he would say about life today):

And the hurrying people daunt me, and their pallid faces haunt me
As they shoulder one another in their rush and nervous haste,
With their eager eyes and greedy, and their stunted forms and weedy,
For townsfolk have no time to grow, they have no time to waste.

Read that last line again. Paterson says that people "have no time to grow" because "they have no time to waste." Paterson was on to something. My own experience of recovering from severe anxiety problems bears this out. I am at my healthiest (and, incidentally, my most productive) when I am not in a hurry.

I turn the idea of missing out on its head by asking myself, "What will I miss out on if I rush?" This is because so much of what life has to offer requires me to slow down rather than speed up to benefit. The tortoise always beats the hare eventually, anyway.

3. Be organised

Being organised minimises unnecessary stress. This is especially true in this age where there is so much to juggle and seemingly so little time to breathe.

I liken the brain's operating capacity to working memory in a computer (RAM). If I ask my laptop to do too many things at once, it reaches a threshold before it begins to slow down the speed at which it does everything. This is because my computer has only so much RAM. The same goes for the brain's pre-frontal cortex, where critical thinking and decision-making take place.

In my experience, being poorly organised leads to having too many "open loops" going on in my mind at once, and soon I feel overwhelmed, losing confidence and focus.

To avoid being overwhelmed, break down whatever you are doing into pieces and just focus on the next step. It doesn't matter your challenge—there is always a next step.

One example of how I reduce the burden on my brain's working memory is by setting reminders. I like to use the personal calendar on my mobile phone to remind me of appointments and errands I need to run. I take the same approach with my work calendar for meetings and upcoming deadlines.

I believe having an awareness of how you are spending your time and consciously making decisions that ensure you are healthily occupied is essential for anybody's mental health. Anxiety thrives on a lack of confidence and clarity about how we are spending our time. Simple things such as a well-kept diary/calendar and a daily or weekly to-do list can be beneficial here.

Everyone's personality has differing levels of comfort when it comes to organising themselves, but to whatever degree is practical for you, it is worth investing time into this.

4. Be digitally wise

It has been my experience that technology is a double-edged sword for my well-being. On the one hand, it enables me to do things I wouldn't have dreamed of growing up, such as playing any song I want for free whenever I want. Cue memories of sitting by the radio hoping to hear my latest favourite hit!

Yet, while technology is an excellent servant, it is also a lousy master. In the digital age, it is easy to treat the mobile phone as simply an extension of your hand, constantly checking emails and news and scrolling social media feeds. If you're not careful, this tendency can put the mind in a constant state of distraction, which makes it difficult, if not impossible, to focus.

The challenge for us all is the digital tools that help us stay connected to each other, do our work and learn new things also place relentless demands on our attention, which can pull us away from what we want or need to do.

In *Your Brain At Work*, David Rock notes, "A study done at the University of London found that constant emailing and text-messaging reduces mental capability by an average of ten points on an IQ test. It was five points for women, and fifteen points for men. This effect is similar to missing a night's sleep. For men, it's around three times more than the effect of smoking cannabis."

I find that using social media can easily make me anxious, and I therefore limit my use. It is undoubtedly a mental health danger zone when it comes to things like body image, politics, and other topics that affect one personally. I have learned the hard way about the negative impact social media can have on my mental health from posting opinions too hastily on controversial topics, which have drawn the ire of others and resulted in pain for me and for them. These days, I am much more careful.

Here are my two cents for anyone looking for guidance on preventing technology-induced anxiety:

- In your free time, be deliberate about what you are doing and learn when is a good time to be on your phone and when is not. A rule of thumb I go by is that if I pull out my phone without having something specific I want to do on it, then I am probably going to end up mindlessly scrolling my personal email inbox or social media, which is neither satisfying nor enjoyable.

- In your work or study time, watch out for digital distractions, including things like email requests or instant messages from colleagues that need to be managed well. Otherwise, they will fill you with unnecessary urgency and contribute to anxiety.

David Rock notes, "The challenge is that any distraction, however small, diverts your attention. It then takes effort to shift your attention back to where it was before the distraction… Distractions are not just frustrating; they can be exhausting. By the time you get back to where you were, your ability to stay focused goes down even further."

This is where prioritising well and blocking out time in your calendar to focus on work that requires your full attention can boost your productivity and mental health.

It's all about being the master of your attention, whether you are working, relaxing or whatever you are doing. If you aren't in control of it, social media algorithms and demanding work colleagues will make sure they are instead.

5. Exit the rat race

I recommend going against the grain of the culture in which many of us live, which promotes the idea that having a crazy busy, run-off-my-feet life-style is to be admired and even striven for. Withdraw from competing with workmates, friends and family members for the title of who has the most exhausting life.

Some years ago, I interviewed a well-known sports commentator who had recovered from a mental breakdown. During his recovery, he realised he had neglected to spend time with his son because he was a workaholic (to the point of accruing over 100 days of annual leave by never taking holidays). He has found it incredibly fulfilling since then to rearrange his priorities.

That might be an extreme case, but we can all learn from it. No one on their deathbed wishes they had worked more overtime.

6. Take rest seriously

Quality rest can be hard to come by, but we all need it. This encompasses far more than sleep.

In her book *Sacred Rest: Recover Your Life, Renew Your Energy, Restore Your Sanity*, American physician Dr Saundra Dalton-Smith says, "Rest is not for weaklings. Hollowing out space for rest is work. Finding time for rest is the hands and feet of the promises we long to claim. It means saying no. It means placing limits on ourselves. It means having limits with others. It takes courage to rest in the midst of an outcome-driven society. It takes strength to walk away from good in pursuit of better."

She explains that there are seven types of rest that everyone needs:

1. Physical rest: This includes sleep, naps, and restorative activities that improve circulation, such as stretching, yoga and massage therapy.

2. Mental rest: It is when you switch off from work and other stress-inducing activities so your brain gets a break from being 'on' all the time.

3. Sensory rest: This is time away from phones, laptops, TV screens and noisy environments.

4. Creative rest: You can find this by taking in the beauty of a pleasant view, walking in a park, or having pictures of artwork and loved ones in your office or home that you can look at to help you reflect and recharge.

5. Emotional rest: This type of rest, where you make time for yourself, is especially important if you are someone others depend on for emotional support, such as a parent or team leader at work.

6. Social rest: This type of rest aims to spend time with people you look forward to seeing and who give you energy rather than taking it.

7. Spiritual rest: This is about transcending the physical and mental so you feel a deep sense of love, belonging, purpose, and acceptance. It requires engaging in something greater than yourself by adding prayer, meditation, or community involvement to your routine.

This is the perfect entree to the next part of the book, which is all about the spiritual aspect of mental recovery and ongoing wellness, which I see as vital to personal growth.

PART 4
THE SPIRIT

Spiritual beliefs and practices are often overlooked, if not completely ignored, in so much of what is out there about mental health and wellness. They have been central to me, as I know they are for many people. I wouldn't want anyone to conclude that because of my difficulties with religious concepts, it must follow that keeping one's faith at a distance is desirable or, indeed, necessary for good mental health.

As I recounted earlier, my religious beliefs got caught up in my mental problems. In those weeks in hospital, as my body and mind started to recover, I decided to focus on what I knew to be true about the character of the Christian God, which I concluded to be one of goodness and sacrificial love for his creation.

Coming at just the right time, this focus put everything else troubling me about concepts like predestination into proper perspective. Remarkably, the troubling thoughts and compulsive behaviours surrounding these concepts melted away during those weeks in hospital after I was diagnosed. From there, I was able to resume practising my faith healthily.

This part of the book remains entirely relevant if you are an atheist or agnostic because, in essence, I am talking about one's deepest beliefs and how they inform your thoughts and actions. For me, this involves my Christian faith. Still, I believe my example is valuable regardless of your background since it can help you think about how to manage your own approach to spirituality. And I have plenty to say about aspects of life such as relationships and means of enjoyment that are not typically categorised as spiritual but are nonetheless means of cultivating inner peace and motivation for living.

CHAPTER 9
PRAYER

Prayer is the most basic and accessible of all spiritual activities and is deeply personal. As an act of communication with a higher power or a form of personal reflection, it is a practice that varies significantly among individuals worldwide. While it is often associated with religious observance, prayer can also be observed among individuals who do not follow a particular religious tradition.

To give you a sense of how universal prayer is, even in today's world where religion is seen as being on the wane in Western countries, according to a Pew Research Center report published in 2017, about 27 percent of religiously unaffiliated Americans (i.e., those who identify as atheist, agnostic, or "nothing in particular") reported that they pray daily.

I consider prayer an essential part of my spiritual and mental well-being. Despite this, it is not something that always comes easily to me. If I didn't make time to pray, it would often not happen. But I know how important it is, so I do it every day, even if I don't feel like it. As my soccer coach from high school used to say about practice, "I don't always feel like doing it, but I always feel satisfied at the end." So it is with prayer.

After I was diagnosed, one thing I changed about my prayers was to pray vocally rather than in my head. This is because, during my mental breakdown, there were times I felt unclear about what I was intentionally praying versus what were merely strange thoughts. Since I knew without a doubt that I could control what came out of my mouth, switching to vocal rather than mental prayer resolved this problem. Particularly if you suffer from OCD, I recommend vocalising your prayers if you encounter the same issue (but only if it helps).

One clinically proven aspect of prayer that is good for any person's health is consciously expressing gratitude. It is widely recognised that gratitude practices, including when expressed in prayer, can benefit a person in a few ways. One of these is mental well-being and psychological resilience. Expressing gratitude in prayer can reduce symptoms of depression and anxiety, enhance self-esteem, provide a sense of meaning and purpose, and increase positive emotions, which help you cope with adversity and bounce back from challenging situations.

For me, thanking God is something I feel is necessary to be true to reality, and if you are new to prayer, I would recommend starting there. Everything—from my very existence and the loving family I was born into to all the good in my present-day circumstances—are unearned gifts from God. Even those things I might have played my part in, such as maintaining good mental health, are much more a product of things out of my control than are in it. It seems only fitting to give thanks.

Prayer is just as powerful when it comes to dealing with painful things in our lives. Maybe you didn't grow up in a loving environment, or your current circumstances are not so good. My experience has been that prayer during adversity or in working through difficulties from the past has been especially powerful and a source of healing.

The same is true when it comes to praying for others in difficulty. When I had to move back to the family farm from Sydney in 2004 due to ill health, a lady from church who I didn't know well at the time wrote me a letter to say she would pray for me daily. I believe God was at work through people like her who prayed for me during that time. Catholic theologian Hans Urs von Balthasar explains in his book *Prayer*, "We do not build the kingdom of God on earth by our own efforts (however assisted by grace); the most we can do through genuine prayer, is to make as much room as possible, in ourselves and in the world, for the kingdom of God, so that its energies can go to work."

Reciting prayers such as the Lord's Prayer, the Hail Mary, and The Lord is My Shepherd gives me a feeling of unity with people of faith who have done the same down through the ages. The Apostles' Creed is both a statement of Christian faith and a prayer I love to say while imagining the millions of voices worldwide now and in centuries gone by who have said it. Something about the final lines I find particularly powerful:

I believe in the Holy Spirit,
The holy catholic church,
The communion of saints,
The forgiveness of sins,
The resurrection of the body,
And life everlasting. Amen.

Perhaps it is because it sums up so much of what I believe. Find the prayers that speak to you most and say them often.

However, as much as prayer can fill a person with inspiration and joy, it is a mistake to see these as essential markers of a healthy spiritual life because, over time, prayer will come easily sometimes, and sometimes it won't. In *Introduction to the Spiritual Life*, Brant Pitre says, "Too many people share the widespread misconception that spiritual consolations are the heart of prayer and worship. For this reason, as John of the Cross laments, many souls tragically abandon the spiritual path as soon as their prayer becomes dry… Like Asaph in the psalm, when prayer becomes dry and dark, we are quick to assume that something is wrong or, worse, that God has abandoned us. But nothing could be further from the truth. Like King David, we must keep praying, even in the midst of the night."

The time we live in has much that pulls us away from stillness and prayer. I wrote earlier about the line from the Banjo Paterson poem where he says that people "have no time to grow, they have no time to waste." Writing 100 years later, von Balthasar adds to this sentiment: "'[Saint] Paul's 'we do not know how to pray as we ought' has probably never been as relevant as it is today. We live at a time of spiritual drought. The images of the world which in former times spoke of God have become obscure ciphers and riddles, the words of scripture have been whittled away by rationalistic sceptics, human hearts have been so crushed and trampled on in this age of the robot that they are no longer sure that contemplation is possible."

The best advice I can give to counter today's relentless focus on efficiency and being productive (good though these things are when approached in a balanced manner) is to make time and space for prayer and contemplation. I take comfort in the advice of one of the great spiritual masters, Saint Francis de Sales, who lived in the sixteenth century and says prayer is about quality, not quantity: "Do not hurry along... try to speak from your heart. A single Our Father said with feeling has greater value than many said quickly or hurriedly."

CHAPTER 10
WORSHIP AND COMMUNITY

For me, prayer has gone hand in hand with coming together with others to worship God and be part of a church community. Depending on my stage in life, this has ranged from simply attending church each week to being involved in the ministries surrounding the weekly church service and participating in mid-week small group meetings at someone's home.

Engaging in worship and coming together with others has several emotional and mental health benefits. Here are some ways in which this has positively impacted me.

- Sense of belonging: Worshipping with others has allowed me to connect with like-minded people who share similar values and beliefs. This sense of belonging reduces feelings of isolation, increases social support, and fosters my sense of purpose and identity.

- Emotional support: Worship involves communal prayers, hymns/songs, and rituals that create a supportive environment. Sharing joys and sorrows, being able to express emotions, seeking solace, and receiving encouragement from others have helped me cope with life's challenges and promote my emotional well-being.

- Stress reduction: Church services involve contemplative and reflective readings promoting mindfulness and inner peace. The focus on the spiritual and higher meaning helps me gain perspective, reduce anxiety, and manage stress more effectively.

- Increased resilience: Being part of a worship community offers me a platform to learn from others' experiences, gain wisdom from shared stories, and draw inspiration from role models past and present. This shared wisdom and support have enhanced my ability to navigate life's difficulties and bounce back from adversity.

- Enhanced self-reflection: Worship provides additional opportunities for prayer and contemplation, through which I can engage in a deeper exploration of my own thoughts, values, and beliefs. This process of self-reflection can lead to greater self-awareness, personal growth, and a stronger sense of purpose.

- Hope and optimism: Rituals, sermons/homilies, and church teachings emphasise themes of faith, love, forgiveness, and redemption, which can uplift me and foster a positive mindset. My worship community's collective energy and support inspire me to face challenges with optimism and maintain hope for the future.

- Increased social connections: Engaging in worship creates opportunities for social interaction and building meaningful relationships. Regular attendance at religious services leads to the development of strong social networks, where I find companionship, emotional support, and a sense of belonging. These connections reduce feelings of loneliness and contribute to my overall mental well-being. Most of the enduring friendships in my life have come from being part of a church community.

I should mention that you can freely participate even if you don't believe in God. The various church communities I have been part of—both Protestant and Catholic—have all been ones where anyone is welcome.

It's worth knowing that Catholic parishes typically open their church buildings to the public throughout the week. This allows anyone to go and sit quietly, taking whatever time they need to reflect or pray. I find it to be a setting that enables me to centre myself and walk out of there in a better state than when I came in.

CHAPTER 11
SPIRITUAL READING

Making time to read, listen and/or watch spiritually focused content has gone hand-in-hand for me with prayer and worship as a means of cultivating my inner growth and personal development.

Owing to my belief that the Bible is the word of God, I treat it as the ultimate source of moral and spiritual guidance, with its teachings, stories, and lessons providing the foundation for my Christian faith and practice. Its passages offer me solace during tough times, provide ethical principles for decision-making, and hope and encouragement.

Practically speaking, I couple my quiet time of prayer with a couple of short readings from the Bible, which is a widespread practice for a great many Christians. As a Catholic, I make use of the daily Bible readings which are the same ones read at Catholic masses each day around the world. I find the readings consistently grounding, uplifting, and reassuring of God's love and purpose for humanity.

To be sure, the Bible is a powerful book, and as my pre-diagnosis period showed, there are mental health considerations to be mindful of when reading it. One of the reasons I decided to become Catholic 10 years ago was the balance that one finds in its interpretations of the Bible.

If I take the biblical topic of predestination as an example, rather than definitively stating how it works, the Catholic Church has set boundaries around what one can rightly say about the matter. It affirms the reality of both God's sovereignty and man's free will. I think, regardless of your denomination, leaving it at that is a very good idea.

If you encounter something that troubles you when reading the Bible, don't keep it to yourself. Talk about it with people you trust, and remember that your faith is meant to be a positive part of your life. If it is having the opposite effect, then something is going wrong.

Thanks to the wisdom of the Bible, I now look back at the hardships of that pre-diagnosis period as a time when God was doing a powerful work of grace in me that would bloom in the years to come and for the rest of my life.

One of my favourite lines in the Bible expresses this paradox about suffering and its effect on spiritual growth. In 2 Corinthians chapter 12, Saint Paul says Jesus told him, "My grace is sufficient for you, for my power is made perfect in weakness."

The place I start when I look at this statement is the word "perfect". I think about what God's power being fully realised looks like. The opening of Genesis comes to mind. The creation of the universe. Boom. Uncountable trillions of galaxies. The beginning of life on earth. Every microscopic detail of the design and healthy functioning of every creature that has ever lived. The sheer beauty of the mountains, the oceans, clouds coalescing for a thunderstorm. He saw it, and it was good.

Then I think about the word "weakness". Not moral weakness—Jesus here is not referring to moral weakness but rather weakness in terms of human suffering: sickness, poverty, anguish, grief, and pain. Crucifixion.

With those two things in mind, I start to understand Jesus's response to Paul's appeal for God to remove the difficulty he is dealing with (referred to as a "thorn"—we aren't told exactly what it is).

Instead of simply taking the "thorn" away, Jesus says that his grace is sufficient because his "power is made perfect in weakness." Somehow, human suffering can have a divine power unmatched by anything of human origin.

Just as Jesus's death on the cross appeared to be a defeat, we feel defeated when we suffer. But the truth is actually the opposite. As Jesus showed in rising from the dead, what he endured was the means of God unleashing his redeeming power upon the world.

This is why Jesus tells Paul that his grace is sufficient. It's everything Paul needs because it is the power of God. Paul says: "Therefore I will boast all the more gladly about my weaknesses, so that Christ's power may rest on me. That is why, for Christ's sake, I delight in weaknesses, in insults, in hardships, in persecutions, in difficulties. For when I am weak, then I am strong."

I am not saying that one should seek out suffering. Indeed, God made people to be healthy and to flourish, which is why Jesus couldn't help but heal people everywhere he went. But if you do suffer, take comfort in the purpose God is able to make of it.

The encounter of Jesus with the man born blind in John's Gospel (chapter 9) speaks powerfully on this question of purpose: "As he went along, he saw a man blind from birth. His disciples asked him, 'Rabbi, who sinned, this man or his parents, that he was born blind?' 'Neither this man nor his parents sinned,' said Jesus, 'but this happened so that the works of God might be displayed in him.'"

The good news is that you don't need to have been miraculously healed like the blind man for this to be true for you. I believe that although God did not cause my mental afflictions, he has used them to demonstrate his healing power through my recovery.

Jesus' remedy for depression and anxiety

Jesus is very aware of the afflictions of the mind and not just the body. He teaches me that the key to living confidently with depression and anxiety problems lies not in my own ability but rather in God's provision. He puts it this way in the Gospel of Matthew (chapter 6):

> Therefore I tell you, do not worry about your life, what you will eat or drink; or about your body, what you will wear. Is not life more than food, and the body more than clothes? Look at the birds of the air; they do not sow or reap or store away in barns, and yet your heavenly Father feeds them. Are you not much more valuable than they? ... So do not worry, saying, 'What shall we eat?' or 'What shall we drink?' or 'What shall we wear?' For the pagans run after all these things, and your heavenly Father knows that you need them. *But seek first his kingdom and his righteousness, and all these things will be given to you as well.* Therefore do not worry

about tomorrow, for tomorrow will worry about itself. Each day has enough trouble of its own. [Emphasis mine]

Jesus knows that my greatest need in life is the well-being of my soul, which is why he says to make that my top priority. It has been my experience that when I do that, God takes care of everything else. With my health and well-being, over and above all that I have spoken about regarding mind and body is the steadying power of knowing in my innermost being that the Lord will provide for my every need.

CHAPTER 12
INSPIRATION

The Latin root of the word "inspiration" means "to breathe into" or "to infuse with breath." It was believed that inspiration resulted from the gods or muses "breathing" ideas or creativity into individuals.

Over time, the meaning of inspiration expanded in the English language to encompass the general idea of being mentally stimulated, motivated, or influenced to create or achieve something significant. Today, inspiration refers to a strong feeling of enthusiasm, motivation, or stimulation that prompts creativity, ingenuity, or action. It can be derived from various sources, such as art, nature, experiences, or other individuals.

Sources of inspiration have played a vital role in my recovery journey and ongoing wellness. I consider these to affect me spiritually, even though they are often not explicitly religious.

The power of art

If my experience is any guide, inspiration can come in many forms and from places you don't expect. Things like movies, music and art have been incredibly important in lifting my spirits and helping me persevere through the difficulties of daily life.

The inspiration I have found in certain music, books, films, TV shows and art has been profound and has contributed significantly to my personal growth and understanding of myself and the world around me.

When something I read, watch or listen to strikes a chord with me, it has healing power because it affirms something true, good or beautiful about life and reality.

A few examples illustrate this.

Earlier in this book, I referred to the film *A Beautiful Mind*. I saw parallels with my own life since it portrayed the true story of someone who has a long period of unrecognised psychosis and a journey of recovery that began in hospital. It meant a lot to me when I saw it for the first time, having only just returned to my university studies and not feeling very sure of myself. It validated for me how challenging the previous five years had been, while at the same time lighting the way to what was possible. If someone with the mental afflictions that John Nash had could become a Nobel Prize-winning mathematician, then I could see the sky was the limit for my future.

I mentioned that you can find inspiration in places you don't expect. The best example from my own experience was how I came to be awe-inspired by a painting, even though I am not someone with a natural appreciation for artwork. I first learned about Pablo Picasso's *Guernica* while studying the history of the Spanish Civil War at university. The scene so vividly portrayed in Picasso's mercurial style was the bombing of a civilian village in the Basque region of Spain by Nazi planes in a haunting precursor to the Second World War. The chord it struck with me was the parallel I drew with the 9/11 attacks, which had such an effect on me. For all the differences between the two events in time and place, they were both air bombings of civilians that shocked the world.

I saw *Guernica* at the Reina Sofia Gallery in Madrid, Spain, in 2011. It is a massive painting with its own room. I must have stood there and taken it in for more than an hour. I was amazed at how it spoke of the truth about what took place and could see why it is one of the most famous artworks of the 20th Century.

My last example involves music. Although I never learned an instrument or had musical talent, music has always been a source of enjoyment for me, as it is for most people. In 2012, I saw Matchbox Twenty live in concert when they toured Australia. It was the year I was suffering from restless legs syndrome and insomnia, and I think this heightened how much I enjoyed the concert because of the difficulties going on in my life. It was a special night that I relived by listening to their music in the weeks and months after the concert.

I mention these three examples of human creativity that inspired me because they were significant to me in my recovery journey and demonstrate how valuable these types of experiences can be for anyone.

At the beginning of this book, I spoke about how the space probe Voyager needed to harness the gravity of the planets it visited along the way, and this is how I view the power that these experiences unlocked in me on my life journey.

Periodic things to look forward to and regular means of enjoyment

To be sure, you cannot always predict when you are about to watch a film that will become one of your all-time favourites, nor is it affordable for most of us to frequently travel overseas to see exhibitions or go to live concerts all the time. However, with the right forward planning, you can ensure that you always have periodic things to look forward to and regular means of enjoyment in your day-to-day, which can inspire and unlock motivation to power you on, improving your quality of life. Doing this also sets the scene for the special moments like the three I just described, increasing the chances of them happening.

Turning firstly to regular means of daily enjoyment, this will look different for everyone according to your tastes, but here is what it looks like for me. As I go through these, you will notice that some of these means of enjoyment involve exercise and nutrition, which I discussed earlier in the book. The important thing to note is that these are just examples, and your own preferences and interests may look quite different from mine, but it should help you identify what could work for you.

The first thing I look forward to in the day is my breakfast, which I get the most out of by sitting and eating it without doing other things simultaneously so that I mindfully enjoy it for its own sake. I set myself in a positive frame of mind by saying a brief prayer of thanks beforehand (traditionally known as "saying grace").

If it is a workday, the first thing I do is prioritise what I will work on for the day. I look forward to this because it clearly defines my focus, reduces uncertainty and anxiety about the day, and gives me my next steps for each task. Of course, things may occur that require me to deviate from the plan, but at least I have a roadmap.

Once I have gotten that far, to satisfy my curiosity, I reward myself with a brief look at what is making news in the wider world. Items of interest can be things I return to during my lunch break or other short breaks during the day when needed.

I try to stop properly for lunch by blocking an hour out in my diary. While it's not always possible to take the whole hour, I need at least a half hour, even on hectic days, to perform at my best in the afternoon. As with breakfast, I sit and eat without doing much else so that I can mindfully enjoy the meal.

I exercise as often as I can after work since I enjoy it and it makes me feel good (there are plenty of people who prefer to exercise first thing in the morning or at other times of the day). In my current stage of life, this happens about three times a week since my parenting duties are still quite intense while our four kids are young.

The evening meal is another daily highlight. My wife and I intentionally sit down to eat and catch up with each other as best we can. Part two of this catch-up and unwinding time is after we have managed to get the kids to bed. We watch a TV series or movie for about a half hour before we each make time for reflection and prayer before bed. I love to read books in bed, which is the last of my daily activities before I sleep.

Weekends form a particularly important part of what I look forward to in order to stay motivated during the week. Taking the kids to sports or other outdoor activities always makes me feel good and like I am part of the local community. This is also true for attending church, which meets my spiritual needs, as described earlier. Other highlights are reading the weekend newspaper, getting takeaway dinner on Saturday nights, and, for me (as a sports fan), watching or listening to a broadcast of a Canberra Raiders game during football season.

You can see from my examples that I leverage many means of enjoyment to manage my daily mental well-being. Being strategic with how I intersperse these into my day and week maximises how positive, motivated and steady I feel.

Planning things to look forward to that happen beyond the daily and weekly cycle is equally important to generating inspiration and motivation.

Vacations are a prime example. Everyone benefits from having a change of scene where you go somewhere near or far from where you live to have a break from the daily grind. Depending on your circumstances, it can be as short as a weekend getaway or as long as several weeks.

Vacations allow you to refresh yourself and enjoy the sights, sounds and experiences of the place you are going. They are also a setting for memorable moments like my *Guernica* experience, which can inspire you long after the vacation is over.

I make sure to catch up with friends and family with whom I enjoy spending time periodically, and once booked in, they can be another thing to look forward to. Of course, there's no reason these can't be an element of your weekly routine—there is a blurry line between the things I consider "regular" and "periodic".

Celebrations are another potential goldmine for inspiration and motivation. I am thinking here of birthdays, anniversaries, weddings, baptisms, milestones and special events like a concert—the list is long and differs from person to person. To be sure, events like these are not always stress-free, but I am thinking particularly of the ones you look forward to and how you can harness their gravity in the lead-up and also afterwards with the good memories.

While I have been focusing here on the value of forward planning, there are also unplanned occurrences that can bring joy and inspiration. I am thinking here of things like running into an old friend, finding a funny clip on YouTube, or spontaneously deciding to go on a picnic. I have found that these can all lift my spirits, and you get the best out of these opportunities if you are mindful and aware of the possibilities around you.

Relationships

The quality of our relationships is a defining factor in our health and well-being. Even the most introverted people need healthy relationships with others to be well and stay motivated.

This is a vital point, especially at a time when a loneliness epidemic is sweeping the developed world.

I am no relationship expert, but I can attest to how important the people in my life are to inspiring and motivating me. If, like me, you have a spouse and children, then these are the most important people in your life.

Don't allow yourself to feel weighed down by being depended on. Rather, let that motivate you. What a privilege it is to be so critically important to another person! I have found that being mindful and regularly praying for my family cultivates my love for them and grounds me in the truth of the beautiful people they are. This inspires and motivates me.

Remember Dr Saundra Dalton-Smith's 7 types of rest I referred to earlier? One of them is "social rest", which is about spending time with people that you look forward to seeing and who give you energy. Everyone needs company like this, so make sure you prioritise spending time with good friends. Men are typically not as good at being organised with social commitments, but I have found it is worth the time and effort to plan these.

Relationships with pets can also play a vital role in someone's health and well-being. The advantages include:

- Companionship and emotional support: Pets offer unconditional love and non-judgmental support, providing comfort during times of distress and loneliness.

- Reduced stress and anxiety: Interacting with pets has been shown to lower stress and anxiety levels. The tactile experience of petting an animal can release oxytocin, a hormone associated with relaxation and bonding.

- Social support and connection: Pets can facilitate social interactions with others and be a positive addition in family settings.

- Sense of responsibility and purpose: Caring for a pet can instil routines and focus, contributing to improved self-esteem and a sense of accomplishment.

- Improved mood and mental well-being: Pets bring joy, laughter, and positive experiences, which can alleviate symptoms of depression and enhance happiness.

If you are considering getting a pet, make sure you think it through and don't make the decision on a whim. Most pets need plenty of attention, and you want to have confidence that they will improve your quality of life, not reduce it.

Two poles to live by

To round out the discussion about inspiration, I want to advocate for two virtues that have been central to lighting the way forward for me: truth and love.

In one of the best-known passages of the New Testament, Saint Paul says in 1 Corinthians chapter 13, "Love is patient, love is kind. It does not envy, it does not boast, it is not proud. It does not dishonour others, it is not self-seeking, it is not easily angered, it keeps no record of wrongs. Love does not delight in evil but rejoices with the truth."

These two virtues complement and reinforce each other. Truth without love can lead to harshness or insensitivity, while love without truth can be misguided and ultimately harmful. Combining truth and love allows for honest and compassionate interactions, healthy relationships, and a more harmonious society.

What Saint Paul says next is truly profound for anyone who has experienced severe mental illness, "[Love] always protects, always trusts, always hopes, always perseveres. Love never fails."

Living confidently with conditions like bipolar disorder and OCD involves plenty of trusting, hoping and persevering. I pray these words may inspire you in all seasons as they have done for me.

CHAPTER 13
GO FORTH

Lives of great men all remind us
We can make our lives sublime,
And, departing, leave behind us
Footprints on the sands of time;
Footprints, that perhaps another,
Sailing o'er life's solemn main,
A forlorn and shipwrecked brother,
Seeing, shall take heart again.
Let us, then, be up and doing,
With a heart for any fate;
Still achieving, still pursuing,
Learn to labor and to wait.

– Henry Wadsworth Longfellow, 'A Psalm of Life'

In closing, I want to return to the place where my recovery began and encourage you to reflect on where you are in your journey.

Freshly diagnosed and sitting in my hospital room doing the mindfulness exercise, I had my first glimpse of what a healthy mind feels like after a lengthy period of pain and confusion. The possibilities seemed immense—and they were.

The path of recovery is not linear. It's filled with twists and turns, highs and lows, but don't let that faze you. There will be moments of doubt and perhaps moments when you feel like you are back at square one. Remember the importance of mindset. "This too shall pass."

No matter what kind of day you are having, you can always do something positive (or refrain from doing something negative) to help look after your body, whether that involves nutrition, sleep or exercise.

The human spirit's capacity for transformation is universal. Recovery is not just about managing your condition; it's about finding a purpose that transcends your struggles. Let your faith, passions and connections with others be guiding lights.

The challenges you face today can become your sources of strength and resilience tomorrow. That is what I see when I look back at myself in the hospital all those years ago.

The future is bright. Go forth!

ABOUT THE AUTHOR

W.B. Turner grew up on his family's sheep farm in regional New South Wales. As a boy he loved playing cricket and basketball, and found his best results at school came from a love of writing—particularly in the subjects of English and History.

Soon after he finished high school, he experienced depression and anxiety which led, after a long period of being undiagnosed, to an eight-week stay in psychiatric hospital in his early twenties. With the benefit of an accurate diagnosis during his hospital admission and supportive family and friends, he completed a degree in media and communications from the University of Sydney and has worked in that field ever since.

As someone with lived experience of both a mood disorder (bipolar disorder) and an anxiety disorder (obsessive compulsive disorder), he knows how living with conditions like these can damage one's confidence and is passionate about encouraging others with mental health issues. He has previously worked as a patient advocate in the New South Wales hospital system and as a volunteer presenter for the Black Dog Institute's high school mental health program.

He lives with his wife and four children in Sydney, Australia.

Visit wbturner.com for more original content by W.B. Turner

URGENT PLEA!

Thank You For Reading My Book!

I really appreciate all of your feedback and
I love hearing what you have to say.

I need your input to make the next version of this
book (and my future books) better.

Please take two minutes now to leave a helpful review online (from wherever you made your purchase) letting me know what you thought of
the book.

Thanks so much!

- W.B. Turner